haverford town *.p*
free library

1601 Darby Road
Havertown, PA 19083
610-446-3082

library@haverfordlibrary.org
www.haverfordlibrary.org

**Your receipt lists your
materials and due dates**

Online renewals at
www.haverfordlibrary.org

"Team Clock is a perfect step up for students of team dynamics who are ready for a thought provoking framework that goes beyond the basic model of 'forming, storming, norming and performing.' Ritter's work provides insight into group behavior and effectiveness, and the natural way groups evolve and grow over time. *Team Clock* is full of applications for every kind of group, from business teams to families."

Professor Julie Hennessy, Clinical Professor of Marketing, Kellogg Graduate School of Management, Northwestern University

"Team Clock provides teams with a direction for future growth".

Dean Simpkins, Director, Football Coaching International

"Team Clock is a brief and unique analysis of the psychology of successful teaming. Through storytelling, case studies and graphics, Steve Ritter offers the reader a specific model and strategies for achieving effective teams – whether in sports, business or schools. Throughout the book, Ritter emphasizes the need for skilled team work if optimum success is to be achieved. In an era when 'professional learning communities' are emphasized as the bases for successful schools, Ritter's book is a valuable tool in teaching the essentials of how these communities might successfully be implemented."

Joanne Rooney, Ed.D., Co-Director, Midwest Principals Center

TEAM CLOCK ™

TEAM

A Guide to Breakthrough Teams

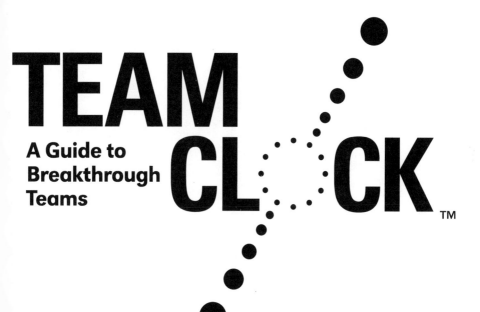

CL CK ™

Steve Ritter

Published by Mawi MawiBooks.com

Publisher's Cataloging-in-Publication

Ritter, Steve.

Team Clock: A Guide to Breakthrough Teams / author Steve Ritter. 1st ed.

ISBN: 9780-9743901-9-2

1. Ritter, Steve 2. Teams 3.Team Success. 4. Team Development.

Printed in the United States of America

Interior and exterior design by Dan Elliott – ligaturestudio.com
Author Photo by Tom Lindfors

Team Clock is dedicated to my family –
the most powerful team in my life.

Thank you Nancy, Meghan, Alissa, and Will
for all you teach me every day.

Contents

Introduction

In 1983, The Chicago White Sox came within one game of winning the American League championship of Major League Baseball. With the majority of the roster returning, most experts predicted a strong 1984 season. By the end of April, however, the Sox were 6-13 after losing five straight games. As a life-long Sox fan, I was having a difficult spring. Deeply invested in the team, I followed them closely. I observed the way they managed victories and losses. I watched the way they handled adversity and disappointment. I scrutinized their responses to media pressure. As a fan, I was deflated, but as a licensed social worker, I was intrigued.

I couldn't help looking for a clinical explanation for why my team was underperforming. It seemed there was something going on that was different than a typical rough start to a season. Players ambled slowly to and from the batter's box. Teammates passively sat in the dugout. When questioned by reporters, players and coaches responded in monotones. The Sox weren't just statistically depressed, they were emotionally drained.

On Monday April 30, 1984, I was having lunch with a colleague, and fellow White Sox fan, at the family services

agency in suburban Chicago where we were both employed.
Commiserating about the Sox over lunch had become our daily
routine. In a workplace full of Cubs fans, the two of us were
relegated to my cramped office to exchange reactions to last
night's game or that morning's sports section of the newspaper.
Between bites of our sandwiches, we dissected the season and
second-guessed the manager's decisions.

As we bantered, the professional therapist side of me kicked
in. "I know what's wrong with the team!" I declared. My friend
laughed and dared me to call the White Sox' General Manager to
offer my diagnosis. I took the dare.

In the years prior to voicemail, a switchboard operator
answered my call.

"Chicago White Sox," she said.

"I'd like to speak with the General Manager of the White Sox,
Roland Hemond," I replied.

"Just a minute, please," said the operator. My stomach dropped
as I realized I was really about to speak with Roland Hemond.

"Hello," said Mr. Hemond.

"Um...uh...," I stuttered. "I'm...um...I'm Steve Ritter,
and...ah...I think I know what's wrong with your team."

"Go ahead," barked Hemond.

"It looks like...well...it seems...," I stammered.

"I think the whole team is...depressed."

For what seemed like forever, the other end of the phone
went silent.

"Mr. Hemond?"

More silence.

"Can you meet me for lunch?" Hemond responded.

"When?" I asked.

"1:00," he replied.

"Where?" I asked.

"Greek Islands...Halsted," he replied.

Click.

Stunned, I looked at my friend in disbelief as I hung up the phone. It was now about 12:30 p.m., and I was scheduled to conduct a therapy group in a half hour. My friend agreed to cover for me, and I pointed my car in the direction of the Greek Islands Restaurant.

Looking back, I'm not sure what gave me the courage to call Roland Hemond, but when a Major League General Manager asks you to lunch, you go. Giddy like a starstruck adolescent, all I remember from my drive to the restaurant was the constant thought pounding through my head, *I just got a meeting with the General Manager of The Chicago White Sox!* Somehow, I managed to get my car to 200 S. Halsted Street where I parked, took a deep breath, and braced for my big moment.

As I entered the restaurant, I spotted Mr. Hemond sitting alone at a table away from the lunch crowd. I noticed he was studying a set of index cards containing the rosters of other Major League Baseball teams. As I got closer, I realized he must be doing what most General Managers do during losing streaks: sort through lists of players in search of a trade that might improve the team.

I joined his table, introduced myself and prepared to substantiate my diagnostic claim based on the numerous observations I had collected during the first month of the season.

"Good afternoon, Mr. Hemond," I began. "I'm the guy who called you about..."

17

Before I could finish my sentence, he stood and offered a handshake. Motioning for me to sit, he gathered the cards from the table and explained that he was, in fact, reviewing trade options. The two of us sat next to each other at a small round table intended for a party of four. I inhaled to speak, but Mr. Hemond held up his hand to indicate he wanted to speak first. Somberly, he revealed that the team had indeed been depressed.

He explained how baseball teams are like families. The players and coaches go weeks and months without seeing their loved ones. As a result, the coaches become like surrogate parents to the players. His eyes began to tear up as he shared that just weeks before the start of the season, two of the team's elders were diagnosed with aggressive forms of cancer and passed away suddenly. Hitting Coach Charlie Lau and first base coach Loren Babe had been deeply attached to the entire team. Their unexpected and abrupt loss had knocked the wind out of everyone.

As I felt the weight of his story, the White Sox' mediocre performance on the field made sense. The team was grieving a significant loss; no trade negotiation was going to change that. We talked for a long time about the nature of loss and the impact death has on families. At the end of our conversation, Mr. Hemond asked if I would consider being the team psychologist. The cross-town rival Cubs had recently hired a psychologist charged with training players to relax at the plate and improve their performance through imagery. The local media had eagerly chronicled these activities over the past few weeks.

Would I consider being the team psychologist?! The giddy adolescent in my head was screaming, *Yes, of course I want to be the team psychologist!* However, the licensed, credentialed social worker in me replied, "These kinds of situations are better handled quietly. Perhaps you and I can guide things from behind the scenes."

Mr. Hemond and I discussed a strategy for assisting the players and coaches with processing the emotions that accompany loss. We talked about this team's clubhouse culture and identified natural team leaders. Some, like manager Tony LaRussa and catcher Carlton Fisk, were more vocal leaders. Others, like outfielder Harold Baines, were less boisterous but just as respected.

Mr. Hemond and I created a plan for coaching the verbal players to lead clubhouse discussions, while silent leaders would let their actions speak. Since everyone manages loss in their own time and their own way, we designed an approach that would be respectful of these differences.

I assured Mr. Hemond that his team's response to loss was normal; as they worked through the grieving process, they would be equipped to make full use of their strength on the field. We agreed to stay in touch throughout the season to monitor the team's progress. Numerous phone calls and letters were exchanged between us as the season unfolded.

The 1984 season leveled out. Following a .381 winning percentage in April, the White Sox rebounded to a .519 winning percentage in May, followed by .536 in June. On August 26, 1984, Chicago Tribune sports columnist Jerome Holtzman interviewed team owner Jerry Reinsdorf regarding the unexpected struggle characterizing the beginning of the season. Reinsdorf was quoted as saying, "I believe the biggest single cause of our decline was the death of Charlie Lau. We miss him terribly."

DEVELOPING THE TEAM CLOCK

My experience with the White Sox fueled in me a quest to understand team psychology. A few years prior to my encounter with Roland Hemond, I had studied group psychology in my graduate social work courses at Loyola University of Chicago. Since the 1960's, traditional models taught that groups must go through a series of phases to manage challenges and deliver results. One of the more popular models, developed by Bruce Tuckman in 1965, describes a sequential process with four stages: forming, storming, norming and performing. Tuckman's model explains that teams gather around a common goal, engage in conflict, establish consensus, and become competent.

While I liked this model, it struck me as having one key limitation: It was too linear. In my experience, teams functioned cyclically. Life's unexpected twists and turns required constant adaptation that could not be measured by any straight line trajectory. Experiences like the Chicago White Sox only reinforced my belief that teams required a more dynamic model.

For the last twenty-five years, I have studied the rhythms, personalities, themes and patterns that come together to make teams work. The result of my research is a simple yet powerful tool I call the Team Clock™.

In the following pages, I will show you how the Team Clock can help you forge more satisfying and effective partnerships. Many clients and friends have told me the Team Clock has helped them become better leaders and teammates. I hope it will do the same for you.

Chapter One
What is TEAM CLOCK?

Although you may not have millions of dollars in sports contracts resting on your team's performance, team success is vital for thriving in every area of life. Like me, you probably find yourself on a variety of teams. By day, I am the human resources director for a financial company. By night, I teach at a local college. On the weekends I play in a community soccer league or have band practice with my buddies. For over thirty years, my wife and I have partnered in marriage and raised three children.

Consider the teams in your own life, using the following definition: *A team is two or more people who collaborate.* Your teams might include your family, your colleagues at work or school, strangers in a pickup game of basketball, or fellow parishioners at your place of worship.

Now consider this question: What is required for a team's collaboration to be successful?

Growing up, most of us are taught how to succeed as individuals. We learn how to set goals, take initiative, and budget our time. When it comes to teams, we tend to apply the same rubric: Skill, respect for others, and work ethic largely determine success.

But as the Chicago White Sox story demonstrates, individual talent and dedication alone are not nearly enough to ensure a team's success. Teams are messy. Conflict is unavoidable. Team dynamics are fluid, ever-changing according to the circumstances, thoughts and emotions of each team member.

Even seasoned business leaders, when asked about the most challenging aspect of their job, regularly cite the management of teams. Graduates of top-tier MBA programs are usually strong individual performers but often struggle in team contexts. In the realm of education, leading a classroom or a school perplexes many teachers and principals.

Despite the challenges, working in teams is fundamental to most endeavors. Teams leverage the talents of diverse people and can generate synergies far beyond the sum of individuals working in isolation.

This book offers a clear model for navigating the complexities of teams. In the Team Clock model, every team is situated somewhere along twelve points that mirror the face of a clock. Understanding the stages of team development and identifying where your team is on the Team Clock can yield new, breakthrough results.

As you will see in the coming pages, the Team Clock has already helped many businesses, schools, athletic organizations, health care operations, families, and interpersonal relationships move past barriers to new levels of success.

Some of the stories I will share with you include:

- Children whose families were going through divorce formed a powerful and effective support group.
- A billion dollar company developed compelling new insights about its culture.
- A struggling elementary school transformed itself into an award-winning school of choice.

The Team Clock will provide you with a clear, concise language you can use to communicate and improve your teams' journeys. As you read on, be sure to think about the teams in your own life and how you might apply the Team Clock.

Chapter Two
Basic TEAM CLOCK

The Team Clock model is a face clock where each hour represents a stage along the path of team development. The key to utilizing the Team Clock is to evaluate where your team is currently situated (or stuck) within the cycle. As you develop a precise picture of where your team is, you will see how to propel your team forward.

These next two chapters will require the most work from you, as you will be learning the Team Clock language. You do not have to memorize every hour – just get a basic sense of how it works and you will know how to apply the Team Clock.

THE CORNERSTONES

Let's begin with the four most prominent points on the Team Clock – what I call the cornerstones: **Attachment** (6:00), **Loss** (12:00), **Dependence** (3:00), and **Independence** (9:00). With these four points, we can explain the basic loop that defines team relationships.

6:00 Attachment

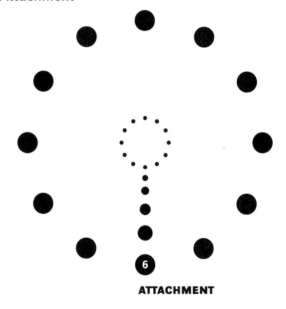

ATTACHMENT

At the base of the Team Clock, in the 6:00 position, is Attachment. All teams seek some level of emotional closeness and unity. At 6:00, team cohesion is so high that individuals feel as one. Closeness is indulged, and we become fully enveloped with our teammates. Of course, attachment feels good, but like most indulgences, it comes with some danger.

12:00 Loss

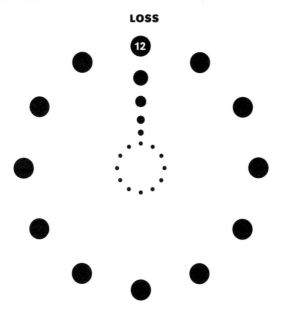

At the opposite end, in the 12:00 position, is Loss. Loss is universal. Each of us has experienced and will continue to endure the sadness of loss. Whether through death, divorce, or departure, people leave our lives. When we've lost someone significant, it's difficult to muster the strength to move forward, even though the world refuses to stop spinning while we recover. Sometimes it's not the loss of a person, but the loss of how things used to be, a loss of status, or a shift in roles and responsibilities.

These first two cornerstones, Attachment and Loss, lead to an important relationship within the Team Clock. **There is a direct correlation between the degree of attachment achieved and the degree of loss experienced within a relationship.**

LOSS

ATTACHMENT

Consider the different levels of attachment in your own relationships. Some of your connections have long and deep histories, while others are more superficial acquaintances. If someone who was only an acquaintance of yours passed away, you would be saddened by the loss but your life may not be impacted significantly. However, other relationships are the product of tremendous investment. Were you to lose these people, a large part of you would feel empty. The world would seem to stop spinning and the depth of grief would trump all other activities in your life.

Each day, we make deliberate choices about the amount of investment we contribute to every relationship on every team of which we are a part. With some relationships, we are cautious with our investment. In these connections, we elect safety over closeness, since a more cautious attachment protects us from the experience of loss. With other relationships, we are willing to cast our fate to the wind and risk the realities of loss in exchange for the benefits of closeness. In these connections, the degree of attachment has no limits since we've already acknowledged and accepted the inevitability of loss.

3:00 Dependence

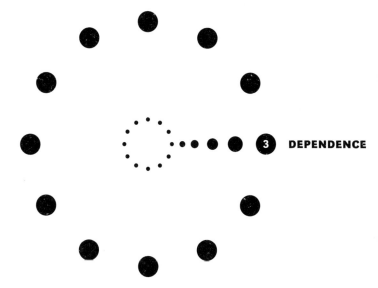

DEPENDENCE

Now, let's look at the horizontal axis of the Team Clock. We'll start with the 3:00 position, Dependence. Dependence is a paradox. On one hand, when we know we can depend on our teammates, we feel a sense of security and safety. On the other hand, our commitment to the team may reduce our level of control.

Imagine someone with his or her hands gently on your shoulders communicating a message of safety. This feels nurturing and makes you want to relax under the comfort of their care.

Now, imagine the same person pressing down on your shoulders, prohibiting you from moving. This action feels oppressive and makes you want to rise up against the force of their control. While we all want to feel safe and secure, few of us wish to feel held down and prevented from growth.

32

9:00 Independence

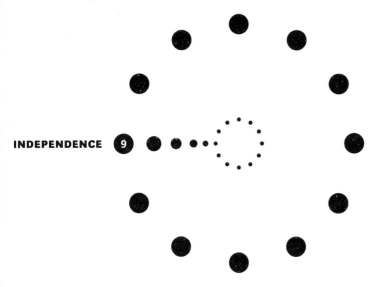

INDEPENDENCE

At the opposite end of the horizontal axis, in the 9:00 position, we find Independence. Independence is both exhilarating and frightening. Similar to 3:00 Dependence, 9:00 Independence requires a delicate balance between freedom and constraint. Being independent means you don't have to rely on anyone else. You can experiment with life seemingly un-tethered from rules and structure. Even in the best of circumstances, however, independence brings apprehension.

Many teens seek independence with relentless energy, even as parents endeavor to set limits. In truth, the independence that promises freedom is linked with the dependence that requires responsible choices. The rebellious teenager who spreads his or her wings is actually practicing the lessons learned when more dependent on others for care. Ideally, the teen grew up being

33

held accountable by his or her parents to make good choices, and gradually internalized those healthy limits and expectations as their own.

These last two cornerstones, Dependence and Independence, lead to another important relationship within the Team Clock. **There is a direct correlation between the degree of dependence achieved and the degree of independence experienced within a relationship.**

In my role as the Clinical Director of a therapeutic day school, I would take students rock climbing and rappelling as a team building exercise. Standing backwards with your feet on the edge of a cliff that drops 200 feet into a ravine is a heart-pounding experience. Even though you are harnessed to secure ropes and have received hours of training, the independent decision to lean backwards off the edge is counter-intuitive. At the moment you allow your body to be given over to gravity, you are immediately confronted with your dependence on the ropes and your training. Thrill and fear are fused as you begin stepping down the face of the rock, seemingly defying the laws of nature. The connection between attachment and loss is crystal clear.

As I learned during my rock climbing expedition, independence requires dependence. The more I was able to rely on my education about technique and proper use of ropes, knots, and grips, the more daring I became. Similarly, a healthy sense of dependence among team members allows individuals to express themselves most freely.

Every day we make deliberate choices about the amount of dependence we accept in each of our relationships. In some relationships, our frustration with the oppressiveness of structure leads us to resist the 3:00 Dependence stage of the Team Clock.

In other relationships, our decision to participate in the labor-intensive phase of building a group structure at 3:00 Dependence, produces the freedom to create, innovate, take risks, and enjoy the fruits of independence at 9:00.

THE FOUR QUADRANTS

Now that we have a general understanding of the cornerstones, we can see what is taking place in each of four quadrants of the Team Clock. Typically, teams begin their journey in the top right quadrant of the clock, in the investment phase.

Investment: Team members invest in a vision for the future with initial caution until a group structure is set. Members test each other to see if they can depend on their teammates. Norms, boundaries and expectations form. Conflict is common. Throughout this phase, members are asking: How much should I invest in this team?

Trust: Members grow more attached to each other and the "way of doing things" that has emerged. Roles, norms, and boundaries solidify. As trust develops, so too does attachment.

Innovation: Investment and trust provide fuel for innovation and healthy risk-taking. At this point in the cycle, members feel free to express themselves. The emerging individuality leads to a sense of independence.

Distancing: A sense of independence prompts members to re-evaluate their position on the team. During this phase, shifts may occur in membership, roles, responsibilities, or group objectives. Members may react by distancing themselves from their teammates and separating themselves from the group's goals. In some cases, this phase signals the end of the team's lifespan. The reason for the team's creation may now be completed and the team will disband. In other instances, this phase simply signals a need for refocusing and readjustment.

Consider the four quadrants using cornerstone terminology. All teams begin with a decision to invest in something new (3:00 Dependence). Trust develops after team members test out their new team and establish a rhythm (6:00 Attachment). This closeness creates opportunities for growth (9:00 Independence). Growth pushes change (12:00 Loss).

TEAM CLOCK AND THE SCHOOL YEAR

One area of life where we see the Team Clock cycle is the school year. The academic calendar has a built-in Team Clock.

As summer comes to an end and autumn begins, students, teachers and parents prepare to invest in a nine-month learning journey. Through the autumn, schools invest in the work of education. This upfront investment yields high levels of trust and learning throughout the winter. As spring awakens, students

37

and teachers wrap up assignments and prepare for a well-earned break. The school year reaches its closing with a commencement, signaling the end of a partnership and the start of something new. In nine short months, everyone has cycled the Team Clock.

Students, parents, teachers, and administrators all renew their investment each autumn. The level of innovation in the spring will depend on the level of investment and trust exhibited in the fall and winter.

VULNERABILITIES

Each quadrant of the Team Clock also possesses certain vulner-abilities. Teams often get stuck when the normal emotions that accompany growth cause stagnation.

Frustration is the normal emotion that occurs when teams wrestle with resistance during the Investment Quadrant. While frustration arising from conflict is healthy and normal, many teams mistake it as a symptom of a problem, rather than leveraging the emotion to solidify values and establish the group's goals. *If a team does not meet conflict head on in the investment stage, the team cannot build high levels of trust or innovation.*

Happiness is the normal emotion felt when teams experience closeness during the Trust Quadrant of the Team Clock. While happiness is a good feeling, it is not always a sign of growth. *Many teams get stuck in the Trust Quadrant because they are unwilling to move beyond their comfort zone to take the risks necessary for breakthrough performance.*

Anxiety is the normal emotion associated with change, as teams navigate the Innovation Quadrant of the Team Clock. During this stage, teams experience the apprehension that comes with courageously stepping beyond their comfort zone. *Anxiety is a sign of growth and functionally necessary for innovation.*

Sadness is the normal emotion experienced when anticipating loss or change in the Distancing Quadrant. While the prospect of separation can be painful, the retreat that accompanies sadness is necessary for the regrouping that inevitably follows a shift. *It is okay and necessary to grieve loss, but we must eventually muster the courage to invest again in our current team or a new one.*

Images are often easier to remember than words. Consider the faces on the Team Clock representing the emotions typically experienced during each quadrant.

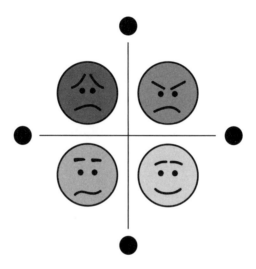

If you're struggling with frustration, it's likely you are confronting different rules and structure than you've previously experienced. If you're feeling happy, you're probably enjoying the closeness that develops when teams are rewarded for their trust. If you are feeling anxiety, you're likely taking a risk or bracing for a change. If you're feeling sad, it's likely you are experiencing a loss of someone or something important to you.

Most teams have patterns of how they respond to the various emotions in each Quadrant. When you think about your own personal themes and patterns, pay closest attention to the places in the cycle where you most commonly get stuck. These are the areas of vulnerability that will benefit most from change.

Are you someone who avoids conflict? Do you prefer to remain in your comfort zone? Does apprehension make you risk-adverse? Have previous losses made you hesitant to face separation? In chapter five of this book, you will see examples of how other teams got stuck and found a path to healthier interactions.

Chapter Three
The Full Clock

Now that you have seen the basic loop, let's look at the full clock. Keep in mind that you do not have to memorize every hour. Just get a sense of how things work.

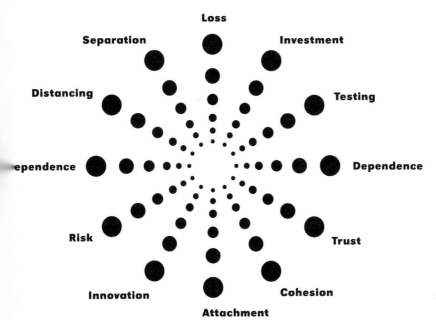

Loss

Separation   Investment

Distancing   Testing

ependence   Dependence

Risk   Trust

Innovation   Cohesion

Attachment

We'll begin at the 1:00 **Investment** stage, since most new connections transition from a prior relationship.

1:00 Investment

Members invest in a new team with initial caution as they strive to decode the written and unwritten rules that govern team interactions. Often the loss of a prior relationship has depleted team members, making it harder to muster the emotional energy to invest.

2:00 Testing

This is a period of careful approach where members further explore what commitment to the team might entail. As members gradually commit, a group structure and rhythm is established that defines the uniqueness of the team. Only after the team has endured the investment and testing stages can they experience the security of the following stage.

3:00 Dependence

At the dependence stage, team members are convinced they can rely on their fellow team members and are committed to the vision of the team. A healthy sense of reliance among team members forges a confidence that will be expressed in the next stage.

4:00 Trust

During the trust stage, members enjoy a sense of closeness and develop the strength to collaborate. When trust is well earned, the team will seem to effortlessly slip into the following stage.

5:00 Cohesion

During the cohesion stage, members begin to think and act as a single unit. This singleness of mind can only be experienced as a reward for the trust built among teammates in the previous stage.

6:00 Attachment

Cohesion that is supported by a strong sense of trust and a healthy level of dependence leads to the elation of unity. At the attachment stage, members identify not only with fellow teammates, but also with the goals of the team.

7:00 Innovation

The unified closeness gives teammates the freedom to express their individuality and to be different. These differences fuel creativity and innovation.

8:00 Risk

The foundation the team has built up to this point supports measured risk, as members are free to try things never before attempted.

9:00 Independence

Benchmarked productivity is the result of a team that has achieved unity and courageously taken healthy risks. Team members are able to act confidently on behalf of the team's goals.

10:00 Distancing

Team members reposition themselves and begin to prepare for changes in the team's structure or focus. Team members often react preemptively by putting space between themselves and other team members.

11:00 Separation

During this stage, the team adjusts according to whatever shifts best support further growth, and participants prepare for transitions in roles.

12:00 Loss

The original composition of the team shifts. The shift is both a loss and an opportunity to invest anew.

THE TEAM CLOCK IN ACTION

Let's look at a specific example of how the full Team Clock works. Early in my career, my work in family service agencies was often guided by community needs assessments. In 1982, the local elementary schools communicated a rise in the occurrence of children of divorce. At the time, school social workers were pressed to provide services to meet the needs of kids from single-parent homes. Community agencies stepped up to assist.

When a coworker and I advertised a twelve-session children-of-divorce group in the summer of 1982, we received more applicants than we could serve. After a careful screening process, we selected eight children to participate in the group therapy. Coming from a diverse array of families, they had almost nothing in common, aside from a recent divorce experience.

Consider again the Team Clock.

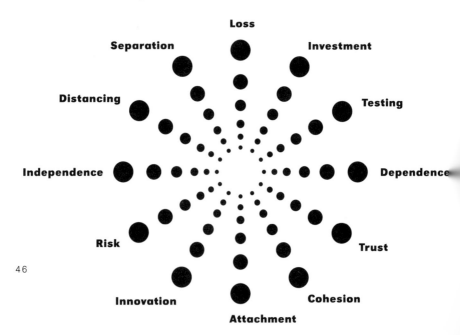

At the **12:00 Loss** stage, all of the children were shell-shocked from the trauma of their parents separating. The children were emotionally depleted. It was hard to imagine what elements would bind them together and give them the courage to discuss their pain. In the **1:00 Investment** stage, the group sessions were awkwardly silent as the kids cautiously measured their commitments. Taking our chances at the **2:00 Testing** stage, my co-leader and I suggested to the kids that the group work together to invent a divorce board game.

Having located a common rhythm at the **3:00 Dependence** stage, the children were provided with all the craft materials they requested, and given the freedom to design the game in any way they wanted, as long as all eight of them agreed. As they tossed around ideas for the game structure, the **4:00 Trust** stage unfolded, and each child offered suggestions based on their own family experience. Gradually, the more confident children encouraged the shy kids, as the **5:00 Cohesion** stage brought closeness to the group. By the **6:00 Attachment** stage, all eight kids were functioning as a single unit, inviting ideas and sharing craft materials. The creativity of the **7:00 Innovation** stage quickly unfolded as the kids drew a path of squares on a large poster board that would be traveled along by rolling dice.

The strength of the team was magnified as the children marked the path of the game board with typical events experienced in divorce such as "Dad gets an apartment," or "Mom goes to court," or "Dad's turn to have us at Christmas." In an act of team bravery, a deck of divorce question cards was piled next to the game board. When a child rolled the dice and was forced to pick a card, a sensitive question had to be answered about his or her

47

own family's experience. Courageously, the children accepted the 8:00 **Risk** stage; these moments usually led to full, in-depth group discussions.

Now in the 9:00 **Independence** stage, as the summer neared its end, the kids fearlessly shared their feelings and spoke excitedly about returning to school in the fall and helping other children with similar struggles. They could now begin to move away from each other in the 10:00 **Distancing** stage, because the structure of the game had provided a platform for supporting emotional pain. At the 11:00 **Separation** stage, the children exchanged goodbyes with a shared sense of pride in what they had accomplished. The kids had used their common bond to create a safe environment for managing change. The Team Clock traveled full cycle to a new 12:00 **Loss** stage from which each child would launch new connections.

I never heard from any of these children following the summer therapy group. I would love to think that life turned out well for each of them. Most likely, however, some or all of them faced new struggles outside the safety of our children-of-divorce group. Hopefully, they met these challenges with a new understanding of their powers to communicate and cope.

As you think about the teams in your own life, consider the following questions: Are you willing to endure the frustration of dependence in order to enjoy the freedom of independence? Are you willing to risk the threat of loss to enjoy the intimacy of attachment? Are you willing to invest labor when you're depleted, so that you can innovate effortlessly when energy is abundant?

Will you extend trust and closeness so that distance and separation are cushioned when things are changing in your life? Where are you on the Team Clock and where are you willing to go?

Chapter Four
TEAM CLOCK Principles

In the next chapter, you will find compelling examples of teams applying the Team Clock. But first let's examine two bedrock principles that make the Team Clock tick. Understanding these principles will help you get the most from the examples.

Team Clock Principle #1: The cyclical pattern is a natural and ongoing part of all relationships.

Teams are always changing because they are comprised of living beings. Living beings, by nature, don't stay the same. Instead of fighting change, healthy teams celebrate change as a continuous and inevitable part of life.

The inevitability of change implies that even life-long relationships do not stay the same. We must be mindful to invest and reinvest in our teams even years after their inception. I think, for example, of an elderly woman who said she had been married seven times, and all seven marriages were to the same man. She explained that every time she and her husband of forty-five years felt the passion in their relationship fading, they took purposeful steps to start "dating" again and got to know the other person as if it was an entirely new relationship. In a way, it was a new relationship each time.

I think also of my experience as a father and my relationship with my children.

Several years ago, I was confronted with the generational realities of having a teenage son. Reflecting on my age, I came to the stark realization that time was short in this important father-son relationship. The foundation of our relationship had long been established, but I found myself wondering whether I had done everything in my power to make the most of our connection.

Somehow the language of childhood wasn't translating into the language of adolescence. Although our relationship was strong, we had come to rely on superficial exchanges in our daily conversations.

"How was your day at school?" I would ask my son.

"Fine," he would reply.

It occurred to me that it was not too late to reinvest in the relationship. Perhaps this stage of our father-son connection required a different approach. That afternoon, while I was driving my son to his weekly piano lesson, I asked him to remove his earphones because I wanted to talk about something. He tried to resist with the classic adolescent deep sigh and eye-roll, and reluctantly turned off his handheld music player. I cleared my throat and offered some thoughts.

"You're getting to the age where hanging out with your dad is not as much fun as hanging out with your friends. As much as I understand that this is a normal part of growing up, I really miss spending time with you," I offered. "Maybe we can have a different kind of relationship now that you spend more time with your friends. Maybe we can use time like this when we're in the car for a half-hour together to catch up on things, instead of me turning on the radio and you putting on your earphones." My son nodded as though to say that he would be okay with this.

Inside, I celebrated at the realization that I now had a weekly 60-minute round trip where I could reconnect with my son! I knew him well as a child, but now I would get a chance to meet him again as a teenager. In the car, my radio was silenced and his music player was put away. Only conversation remained. By the time we arrived home, we had shared a powerful exchange about an awkward peer situation he was managing. The Investment stage of our Team Clock cycle had begun again.

We are continuously going around the Team Clock. Because people change and circumstances change, the relationships that comprise our teams must also change. Whether as a result of planning or happenstance, the addition or subtraction of a member, the success or failure of a project, or simply the next stage of development, every shift alters the rhythm of a team. Strong teams not only accept change, they expect and manage it in a proactive manner.

Team Clock Principle #2: Each stage of the clock is functionally necessary to support the stage opposite to it on the clock. Too often we approach new teams with the unrealistic expectation that cohesion and trust will instantaneously emerge. Fundamental to the Team Clock is the understanding that investment at the front end of relationships is crucial for experiencing the joys of well-developed relationships later on in the cycle.

Recognizing the interplay between the different stages of the Team Clock can help you overcome difficult situations. When you see, for example, that your team cannot achieve high levels of innovation at 7:00 without first doing the hard work of investing at 1:00, it is easier to endure the discomforts of conflict and testing.

Consider the following example that shows how the level of trust built in the 4:00 stage determined the type of distancing team members experienced in the 10:00 stage.

In 2009, many industries were required to take drastic measures to survive a struggling economy. Reduced hours, salary cuts, benefit reductions and layoffs became commonplace. As a human resources director of a small business, I was forced to deliver bad news to 10% of our workforce.

All but two of the workforce reduction discussions proceeded routinely. Two of them, however, stood out as either extraordinarily negative or extraordinarily positive. The difference was predictable. These two employees had made strikingly different contributions at their 4:00 Trust phases of engagement with the organization.

54   The first employee was livid with the news of the layoff. This employee had never gone out of his way to connect with others

in the organization. When invited for lunch or after-hours socialization, he regularly declined. He rarely attended holiday events and offered little personal information to colleagues. As a result, while the employee was accepted as a member of the team, he had built very little mutual trust with his teammates.

Upon learning of the layoff, this employee was visibly furious and created a scene in front of his coworkers. Refusing to participate in the exit interview, he stomped out of the workplace, swearing and criticizing the organization. The lack of trust at 4:00 made distancing tumultuous at the 10:00 stage.

The second employee managed the termination with professionalism and grace. From her first day on the job, she had reached out to coworkers at all levels. She was known for going the extra mile to assist co-workers with projects, and regularly participated in company events. In the middle of the layoff discussion, she interrupted my prepared informational remarks to comment, "How are you doing through all of this? This must be a very difficult day for you too."

As you would expect, the second employee left with a long list of coworkers willing to provide references and recommendations. She quickly located a new job and stays in touch with her former coworkers. Her high level of mutual trust at 4:00 made distancing a more comfortable and positive experience at 10:00.

As we dive into more examples of how the Team Clock works, watch for how these two principles apply: (1) **the cyclical pattern is a natural and ongoing part of all relationships**, and (2) **each stage of the clock is functionally necessary to support the stage opposite to it on the clock.**

Chapter Five
Example Stories

We've all been a part of teams that have experienced failure. Whether it's the breaking of a romantic relationship; family estrangement; misunderstandings among friends; or work-place tension, the ability for humans to not get along is obvious. Hopefully we learn from our mistakes and our wounds; but in the grand scheme of things, it's safe to say some teams are just not meant to be.

There will be times in life when the best move for your team is to disband. The objective that brought you together dissolves, or for various other reasons you find it impossible to progress around the clock. In such cases we feel the heaviness of 12:00 Loss. For every loss we experience, though, there is often another team in our life that is worth our attention: a new relationship, a new job, an old friendship worth renewing, or a frustrating project that with time and dedication could become a success.

The following is a collection of success stories I've gathered over the years, examples where the Team Clock articulated a path for innovation among teammates. Because every team is unique, it's not possible for me to outline every potential application of the model. What I can do, however, is offer real life case studies that will show you how others have referenced Team Clock both in personal and professional contexts.

As you review the examples, be sure to ask yourself the question: Where are my teams on the Team Clock?

LEADING A NEW TEAM

In July of 2005, I received a call from the principal of a Chicago suburban elementary school. A year prior to the call, there had been a controversial transition of leadership. The previous principal was a former teacher who was well respected and endeared for his gentle demeanor and family-friendly style. The buzz around the community was that he would be deployed by the district to another school in town that had lobbied for his leadership. When his departure became official, families and staff took the loss hard.

Neighborhood conversations regarding his transfer and ultimate replacement were rampant. Shortly before the 2004-2005 school year kicked off, the replacement principal was named. She was a young woman with a fresh Ph. D., and she represented an ethnic minority found sparingly in this white, upper-middle-class suburb. Both the families and the school's faculty did their best to manage the transition professionally during the principal's first year, but it was clear that the community still felt the sting of losing their beloved, grandfatherly leader. Although the new principal seemed smart and was clearly committed to academic excellence, she was…well…she was just "different."

The new principal had received my name from one of the teachers on the faculty who was familiar with Team Clock. When the principal called, she expressed concern that the faculty had spent her first year splitting into two factions: those who were still angry about her appointment, and those willing to move forward despite missing their former leader. I agreed to serve as an outside consultant to her team.

For many teams, the most daunting challenge is their lack of a simple, common language that can help them analyze where they are and where they would like to go. While people often instinctively sense when something is going well or poorly, they don't always know how to place their feelings on a continuum within a larger team journey.

Once I taught the Team Clock model to the school's faculty, they had a common language. Loss was explained as a natural part of life. It was normal for the team to mourn the departure of their beloved principal. But eventually, the team would have to reinvest in a new principal. Once they reinvested, they could eventually build trust and get to the point where they were innovating and enjoying their work again.

As part of the investment phase, I asked the team to establish some basic common beliefs. The challenge was to define a consensus philosophy, mission, value set, and vision for the school under the umbrella of the district's overall mission. Initially, we met as a full team where everyone participated in a "Vision Pyramid" exercise. In this task, team members were asked to offer up answers to four questions: **Why do we exist?** (philosophy); **What do we do?** (mission); **How do we do it?** (values); and **What is our goal?** (vision). After gathering an abundance of input, we divided into smaller teams to tackle the task of distilling the responses into collective definitions.

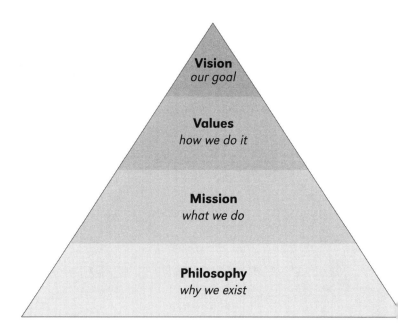

The exercise revealed the core elements of the team's internal differences and forced teammates to engage in productive conflict. As some of the initial brainstorming ideas were shed in favor of simpler language, veteran faculty became attached to their words and unwilling to accept the alternate phrasing offered by newer staff. Contentious yet respectful arguments unfolded. As the struggle around wording continued, the new principal calmly shared an observation.

She said that she had been listening carefully to the team's disagreement and noticed that there was one thing that every point of view had in common: they were all there for the kids. Sometimes, healthy disagreement is the path to consensus. Unified by the principal's insight, the team challenged every word until they had hammered out a complete philosophy, mission, values, and vision statement.

Philosophy: We believe in a safe, positive learning community dedicated to collaboration, professionalism and mutual respect.

Mission: We specialize in engaging all children in an active learning environment that encourages innovation and creativity to empower lifelong success.

Values: Our actions will be guided by integrity, optimism, and unity.

Vision: Together, we are dedicated to the education and development of the whole child.

We then created a behavioral guideline contract that would hold each member of the team accountable for living the agreed-upon values of the organization. Statement by statement, the staff crafted a set of commitments that nearly everyone on the team could embrace. They agreed to hold themselves and each other accountable to the following guidelines on a daily basis:

- Am I a positive role model for students, peers, and community members?
- Do my actions strengthen or weaken the individuals and teams with whom I partner?
- Have I considered other viewpoints from the perspective of those affected by my words and actions?
- Have I conducted myself in a way that is constructive, professional, and respectful?
- Am I committed to pushing myself, my team, and my organization to the next level of excellence?

The team moved through the school year with these commitments. Gradually, behaviors that fell outside of these guidelines were confronted. In most cases, one or two confrontations were enough to prompt a behavioral change.

By the end of the year, it was clear what was required to be a successful member of the team. In a few cases, we had to say goodbye to staff members who repeatedly refused to invest in a healthy manner. Sensing they no longer fit in the new team culture, these staff members pursued other professional opportunities.

As the actions and character of the group increasingly reflected the common language, the team sensed itself entering the trust phase of Team Clock. The primary ground rule was mutual respect. Open-minded debate solidified common objectives. Each day, members would test their new commitment with support, confrontation, and feedback. Conflict was invited, rather than avoided.

Once, a veteran teacher responded to a suggestion by a younger staff member by rolling her eyes. Almost immediately, her peers called her on her non-verbal reaction and asked the younger teacher to further explain her idea. The veteran teacher apologized for being disrespectful. Interaction by interaction, they took steps closer to each other. With each step, the goal became increasingly clear. Each member could see how his or her actions either strengthened or weakened the team's health. Over time, the staff became stronger than ever seen in the history of the school.

Organizational health metrics showed moderate improvement by the end of the 2006 school year. By the end of 2007, the principal and faculty were performing above benchmark. Student test scores rose, and organizational health metrics skyrocketed. Both the new principal and the faculty were widely recognized and celebrated by parents, students, and the community.

The team's success resulted in new opportunities for its members. Most notably, the now widely celebrated principal was recruited as an assistant superintendent by a neighboring district. As fate would have it, the team would again be challenged to adapt as the school welcomed yet another markedly different principal in the fall of the 2007/2008 school year. Once again, the team was reminded that change is inevitable. They would have to invest again under new circumstances.

Key Insights

This story offers the following key takeaways for anyone leading a new team:

- **Language:** Start by establishing a common language for the team's journey.
- **Invest:** Create a framework for investing in one another and building trust.
- **Patience:** Do not rush the journey. Though we all want innovation, investment and trust must come first.

UNDERSTANDING TEAM CULTURE

In 2009, I presented the Team Clock to a sales team for a Chicago-based financial institution. Named one of the top twenty "Best Places to Work" by Crain's Chicago Business, this team was a top performer in a 150-year-old financial services network, boasting over $150 billion in assets and twenty-five consecutive "Most Admired" company rankings by FORTUNE magazine.

Recruiting new salespeople was fundamental to the firm's growth. Accordingly, the Managing Director of the sales team was interested in improving the recruitment capture. For his particular office, the goal was to hire three great new recruits a year. Despite a wide professional network, finding the recruits was a labor-intensive ordeal that required year-round attention.

I presented the Team Clock to key members of their staff one afternoon. We moved around the clock, inviting discussion in response to the following questions.

- How does a new member of a team invest in your culture?

- How is conflict managed during the testing period?
- Once accepted on the team, how is trust evidenced?
- Does the reward of strong team performance match the intensity of the initial investment?
- Does the culture welcome change in roles and membership?
- What happens to recruits who can't live up to the team's high expectations?

Through the discussion, the staff realized that successful recruits were those who could move quickly beyond investment to trust. Why? Because new recruits only had three months to establish a solid sales record. If they spent those three months trying to figure out whether they liked the team, or how much they should invest, it'd be too late to build a strong track record. But if new recruits invested quickly, the firm embraced them with levels of trust and compensation far beyond what most teams would have offered.

The Team Clock offered the team a new, precise language for the kind of journey a successful recruit would need to take. As a result, the team could better communicate opportunities to potential candidates.

As it happened, the next day I was speaking to a colleague whose friend was recently laid off due to a slumping economy. She shared that her friend was coping well with the unexpected departure from his previous job and was eager to re-enter the workforce in a new capacity. As I asked questions about the friend's temperament and talents, it became apparent to me that he embodied many of the qualities the financial firm I'd just presented to was seeking. In particular, the friend had demonstrated an ability to move from an investment to trust phase faster than most people.

As we considered referring her friend to the financial services company, we talked about the differences in the way people approach trust. We both knew people who find it very hard to trust others. Perhaps they have experienced a devastating loss or just have a cautious personality. We both also had acquaintances who trust people easily. Her friend happened to be such a person.

By that evening, contact information had been exchanged between the recruitment director and the potential candidate. Within a week, the candidate was hired and immersed in the firm's orientation and training program. In a process that normally takes four months, the firm was strengthened within days, by virtue of an improved understanding of their culture.

Every team has unique proclivities that shape its culture. The interactions between members are the vehicles for testing trust. Sometimes, casting fate to the wind provides instant membership on the team. Other times, a healthy amount of caution creates safety as the team moves forward. This is a decision that all of us, whether on a sales team or in an interpersonal relationship, need to make.

Key Insights

Using the Team Clock paradigm, a team seeking a new lens for understanding its culture should ask:

- What are the proclivities of our team culture?
  Do we effectively handle loss and move on to investment?
  Do we successfully move from investment to trust?

- Does our team culture make business sense?
  Are our proclivities selected by design or by happenstance?
  What adjustments might we make?
- How can our new understanding of our proclivities inform
  future business decisions such as training, recruiting, and sales?

REDEFINING SUCCESS

I enjoyed my twentieth anniversary as a youth soccer coach in May of 2004. As my children were growing up, I volunteered to coach whatever team my kids were selected for, based on the results of the annual tryouts. In this particular year, the local community soccer club decided to form a team blending the seventh and eighth graders who hadn't made the cut. Hopefully this would ease the kids' disappointment at not making the "select" team that was now populated by their friends from previous teams. I agreed to coach the seventh and eighth grade alternate team.

The initial result was a disaster. Both the kids and their parents still felt the sting of rejection from not making the "select" team. The eighth graders wanted nothing to do with the seventh graders, and the seventh graders were intimidated by having to "play up" in an eighth grade division. We began the season with the lowest team rank in the league.

Either by their own accord or through their parents' influence, a few players quit. The remaining players were handily outmanned in every game. Morale was at an all-time low, despite my best efforts to provide optimistic coaching. Practices were half-hearted; parental involvement reluctant.

67

My Chicago White Sox experience had taught me that talent alone did not determine success. Other sport experiences had taught me the opposite: that even teams with low levels of talent could perform well if they had built trust based on strong, team-wide investment. With my current team, however, players and parents lacked both talent and the desire to invest in each other. And without investment, we could not build trust and cohesion – much less innovate.

I started with the parents. One by one, I asked them what was more important: that their kid plays on the elite team, or that their kid has a healthy, fun experience that builds their confidence and maintains their love for soccer. The parents agreed that they had to redefine their basic paradigm with their kid's own positive development as the end goal.

The players slowly sensed the shift in their parents. After the fifth consecutive loss, it became clear that the team's greatest vulnerability might actually be their greatest strength. Each of the players on the team had been rejected. Each of them had been treated as though they weren't good enough. If nothing else, there was a common goal to prove a few people wrong.

Now that they were invested in a healthy vision, the team could build trust. Linked by their common purpose, the team grew closer. Encouraged by their parents' enthusiasm, the players were driven by an intrinsic commitment to have fun and work together. Communication on and off the field increased. Players began to take risks on the field that took the team to the next level. They began passing the ball, rather than trying to do everything on their own. Although they lost the next four games, the scores were closer and their attitude was positive.

Going into their tenth and final game of the season, the team was at the peak of its chemistry. Our opponents scored early, but we answered with a goal of our own. The score remained tied until the final few minutes, when a series of crisp and accurate passes propelled the ball into the back of the opponent's net for a 2-1 victory. Needless to say, the team finished the season feeling like World Cup champions, despite their 1-9 record.

The story of these inspiring students and parents shows that when we allow ourselves to examine our most basic paradigms, we can often spark new, unimagined growth. Quite often, our greatest problem is not that we've lost something, but rather that we view that loss only as a loss.

Key Insights

If you find yourself on a team that is focused primarily on the loss it is experiencing, ask the following questions:

- Have we considered the possibility that this loss might actually open the door to new opportunities?
- What new attitudes or paradigms would we need to adopt in order to create the possibility of investment, trust, and innovation?
- Do we need to redefine success?

IMPROVING PATIENT CARE

Hospitals traditionally view the patient experience from two separate perspectives: clinical services and support services. Doctors,
nurses, social workers, therapists, and technicians deliver clinical
services. Housekeepers, food service workers, volunteers, trans-
porters, and guest relations employees provide operational support. The single recipient of these two service delivery systems is,
of course, the patient.

In 2004, I was on a team of ten Operations Directors at one
of the nation's leading hospitals. My boss, the Chief Operating
Officer, approached our team with an idea to integrate clinical
and support services. At first, it was hard to imagine how these
divergent teams would mesh.

We began meeting with a single purpose: to forge a common
vision for improving patient care. We examined the vast differences built into the routines of the clinical and support teams.
The clinical professionals were committed to quality medi-
cal outcomes. Physical wellness was the measurement of their
success. The support professionals were committed to service
excellence. Efficiency of service delivery was the measurement
of their success.

Initially, each team instinctively protected the priorities of its
own departments. But we quickly realized that we could not ar-
rive at a common vision without understanding the key elements
of each other's role.

The housekeeper, for instance, gained a better understanding
of the turn-around time needed for the nurse to facilitate expe-
dient patient transfers. The nurse gained a better understanding
of the food service worker's attention to the temperature of the

meal leaving the kitchen as they timed the delivery of the tray to the patient's bedside on the nursing unit. As each of us described the specialties in each department, the overlap was obvious. Every action was designed to meet the needs of the patient. This unified focus became the common vision for our team.

Small actions served to build trust. One morning, a food service worker called the nurse's station to apologize for a late tray delivery and expressed concern for any inconvenience the patient or the nursing staff might have experienced. On another occasion, a nursing supervisor stopped a housekeeper in the hallway to thank him for the quick turn-around following a patient discharge, since the unit was anticipating a difficult patient transfer in that room. Every time our team of Operations Directors met, a new story of collaboration was shared. In time, the desire to help each other became a norm. Previously separate hospital functions were now coordinating their work.

Months later, the reward of everyone's investment began to pay off as innovations unfolded. Housekeeping room turnover times were expedited to enable quick discharges and transfers. Proactive behavioral health interventions prevented routine challenges from becoming emergencies. Nutritionists and nurses partnered in developing a hotel-style room service model. Because our common vision was to integrate services to improve care, patient satisfaction scores improved.

True to healthy team cycles, the professional growth that resulted from our innovations fueled change. I was recruited by another organization that had heard of our transformative work. Saying goodbye to my teammates was difficult as I prepared for my new challenges. All of the directors at the hospital have since moved on to new professional opportunities. The lessons learned from our partnership now strengthen many other organizations.

Key Insights
Differences are often the fuel for team growth. Consider the following when you are integrating diverse teams.

- **Dialogue:** Give team members an opportunity to dialogue openly and develop an understanding of what their teammates do and why they do it.
- **Vision:** Together, create a common vision that meets the needs and aspirations of all stakeholders.
- **Implementation:** Create specific actions that team members can take to implement the new vision. Develop a schedule and success metrics.
- **Celebrate:** Measure and celebrate the small daily actions that will eventually build trust, innovation, and breakthrough levels of performance.

RENEWING A FRIENDSHIP
I shared the Team Clock with my friend Stacey at a time when she was dealing with conflict with her best friend. Not knowing the impact the model had on her situation, she later told me her story.

Karen and I had been best friends since college. For years, she and I were each other's rock. Through all the ups and downs of boyfriends, jobs, and moves, we were each other's closest confidant and biggest cheerleader. We had become like family to each other. In fact, on my health insurance application, she was the only person I gave permission to make life and death decisions for me.

Even though we live thousands of miles apart and our daily lives look vastly different, Karen was a major part of my life. Phone calls, letters, and visits kept our bond close over the years. I was confident our friendship would weather all life's changes.

In our almost ten years of friendship, Karen and I never really fought. Looking back, I can see how we had cycled through the Team Clock several times, but nothing compared to the conflict we faced recently.

Karen had just gotten engaged, when I flew out to visit her for a couple weeks. We spent hours reminiscing about old times, sharing with each other about current struggles, and rejoicing together over her new found love and the exciting future she and her fiancé were planning. Karen asked me to be her Maid of Honor; and I spent the next week helping her shop for a wedding dress.

After I returned home from my visit, Karen sent me an email sharing with me some new details about her and her fiancé's plans. When I questioned the wisdom of their decisions, Karen became uncharacteristically distant and short in her replies. In my mind, I was being protective of her safety and well-being; but in her mind, I was raining on her parade. I wrote Karen a long, heart-felt letter about how much her friendship meant to me and explained that I'd only raised concerns out of love. I didn't hear a word of reply for two months.

During the period of silence between us, I dealt with a lot of emotions. For so long Karen had been a steady part of my life. To not have contact with her — or any sort of resolution — felt like mourning the death of a family member. I looked at the Team Clock model and saw how, shockingly, in only a few short weeks, we had moved from 6:00 Attachment to 11:00 Separation. I desperately wanted our relationship to be restored; but given Karen's unwillingness to communicate, I didn't know how progress was possible. I stared at the 12:00 point on the clock and realized the only thing left for me to do was accept the loss of our friendship.

A few days later, on an uneventful Thursday night, my phone rang. It was Karen. She said she wanted to reconcile and desired our friendship be mended. She apologized for the gap in communication and re-invited me to be part of her wedding party.

If I wasn't familiar with the Team Clock, I think I would have processed my conflict with Karen very differently. I probably wouldn't have been willing to let myself endure the grieving process of losing a friend. And once reconciled, I wouldn't have been as aware of the work needed to rebuild the relationship. I know now that our relationship is like an entirely new friendship. Things can't instantly go back to how they used to be. It's going to take time to rebuild trust in each other; but I am confident that with investment on both our part, we will once again be able to share a closeness that will only be stronger because of the challenges we have endured.

Even for the relationships in our lives that we hope are lifelong teams, the twelve points around the Team Clock hold true. Loss will be experienced in one fashion or another, and a decision to reinvest must be made on the part of all team members.

Key Insights

Stacey's story of her conflict with Karen provides lessons for any interpersonal relationship.

- It is impossible to progress around the clock when a team member is unwilling to invest in the group's progress.
- Changing circumstances outside of a relationship often require corresponding changes within a relationship.

- Conflict and change, when handled correctly, can forge a stronger bond than was previously shared.

LIFE AND DEATH

A few years ago, I received a call from a close friend in rural Minnesota. She was losing her battle with cancer and wanted to say goodbye. The 650 mile drive to her bedside was full of memories of our years as friends. The events and exchanges that populated the history of our friendship ran through my mind.

I played music we had shared during past car rides. I thought about how I would rearrange this year's garden without the wisdom of her yearly horticultural tips. I recalled the things that made us both laugh and cry. As I arrived at her home, I was unprepared to grasp the reality of the ending. This was the lonely aspect of the 12:00 Loss stage of the Team Clock. Apprehension filled my body.

Our final visit lasted about thirty minutes, as the effects of the morphine sent her to sleep. In that half hour, the world stood still. We looked back on our memories. We looked ahead to unknown changes. We exchanged goodbyes. Our original choice to fully attach was rewarded by an ending where nothing was held back.

When I left her bedside, I had a fifteen minute drive to where I was spending the night. It was late and the night sky held the level of darkness that is only experienced in rural areas. The final couple of miles of my trip took place on a winding, one-lane dirt road. I was idling along at about ten miles per hour with my thoughts far away. Without warning, three deer came bounding out of the woods and slammed into the side of my car.

As I slid to a stop, the largest of the three hit the side panel of my driver's side door, creating a moment when the deer and I literally saw eye-to-eye with only a window separating us. The other adult deer bounced off my rear quarter panel leaving surprising amounts of fur and urine as its signature. The third deer was a baby. It couldn't have been in the world for more than a few months. The fawn careened off my hood before regaining its footing, joining his shaken family, and retreating into the woods; all of them seemingly unharmed.

Needless to say, my car was not unharmed. At the moment, however, the damage to my vehicle didn't matter. Life and death had somehow seized the same moment. I completed my brief drive and crawled into bed. I missed my friend deeply, but was somehow soothed by the sight of the family of deer surviving their encounter with my automobile.

I was grateful to be alive. In the midst of deep pain, there were new signs of life to be found. Even in our toughest times, the cycle continues. Whenever we are ready, the loop is always waiting for us to reinvest. We grieve the loss of our loved ones, but can connect with others who will also enrich our lives and offer healing.

Chapter Six
Application

Now that you understand the Team Clock and have seen it applied to a range of teams, let me offer some final thoughts on how you can apply it in your own life.

ACKNOWLEDGE THE CYCLE

The most basic application of Team Clock is the recognition that team development is cyclical and ongoing. Expect your teams to change. Expect to have to go around the loop time and time again. Recognize that grief is as important as happiness, investment as important as innovation.

ESTABLISH A COMMON LANGUAGE

Use the Team Clock as a communication tool to help your teams understand their journeys. Sometimes, just having the language and knowing the basic loop will be enough to inspire breakthroughs. I recently led a workshop for a school superintendent and his leadership team. In the midst of the workshop, the superintendent acknowledged that his team was stuck at 6:00 Attachment. The team was happy; but unfortunately, it had stopped growing.

While other superintendents who struggled with investment and trust looked at him with envy, he explained that, as a leader, he had failed to inspire the team beyond its comfort zone. During the workshop, he challenged his entire team to take new, smart risks.

Like the superintendent, you can propel your own teams in a powerful new direction simply by asking the question: Where are we on the Team Clock? If you feel adventurous, have each team member anonymously write three sentences about where they think the team is, then read everyone's response aloud.

DEVELOP AN ACTION PLAN TO MOVE AROUND THE TEAM CLOCK

In each quadrant, there are some key things you can do to move your team forward:

Investment
- **Vision:** Create a common vision, much like the example of the new principal in Chapter Five. The foundation of a team's ability to trust and take risks will be built upon this vision.
- **Conflict:** Address conflict as an opportunity for growth. Endure the discomfort needed to air all perspectives.

Be willing to acknowledge that sometimes conflict is significant enough that a change in team membership may be appropriate.

- **Routines:** Set a rhythm of routine interactions. Predictable routines create an atmosphere of safety and a platform from which trust can begin to form.
- **Boundaries:** Set clear boundaries. What things are non-negotiable? Teammates should know what is and is not expected of them.
- **Norms:** Encourage healthy norms and cutoff unhealthy norms. Norms encompass obvious things such as the length of lunch breaks and more nuanced things such as the language used by teammates.

Trust

- **Take Small Actions:** Small, consistent actions build trust.
- **Be Direct:** Be direct and frank, while maintaining a respectful tone.
- **Enforce the Vision:** Do not let isolated individuals destroy the vision. Confront inappropriate behavior head on.
- **Earn trust:** The only way to achieve closeness is for team members to continuously take steps closer to one another.
- **Review:** Take time to reflect and review the norms, routines, and boundaries that have emerged. Do they make sense? Do any need to be adjusted?

Innovation

- **Incentives:** Reward people for smart risk-taking, even when they fail.
- **Encouragement:** Laud initiative and creativity.
- **Diversity:** Encourage diverse points of view. Allow for anonymous feedback.
- **Improvement:** Challenge team members to never sit on their laurels. Seek continuous improvement.
- **Resources:** Dedicate time and capital resources to new ideas.

Distancing

- **Mourn:** Give yourself room to grieve as appropriate.
- **Duration:** Do not mourn forever. Muster the courage to invest again.
- **Adapt:** Keep your eyes open. Often, the end of a relationship signals the beginning of a new opportunity.

If you've skipped a quadrant, go back and repeat it. For example, if team members don't have much trust for each other, go back to the investment quadrant and look at vision, boundaries, norms, and conflict. If team members resist innovation, see if you can invest or build trust in ways that better support innovation.

Together as a team, envision your ideal path through the Team Clock. Recognize the functional value of frustration, happiness, anxiety, and sadness.

ADDITIONAL RESOURCES

If you want to learn more about the Team Clock, please visit us at www.team-clock.com. We offer many additional resources including:

- Consulting services where our licensed facilitators work directly with your team.
- In-depth guides to navigating each stage of the Team Clock.
- Team Clock exercises and workbooks for improving team performance.

We welcome your feedback. By sharing both positive and constructive thoughts, you can help us move to the innovation stage of our own Team Clock.

Afterword

When The Chicago White Sox won the World Series in 2005, twenty years had passed since my initial meeting with Roland Hemond. In 1985, Roland had sent me an autographed photo of my daughter's favorite player, Harold Baines, accompanied with a note saying, "I wish I could see the look on your daughter's face when she receives this." Two decades later, Roland had the chance to see my daughter face to face.

My daughter and I reconnected with Roland at the 2005 annual winter "Soxfest." Roland and I reminisced about our happenstance encounter in 1984 and laughed about the turn of events that had culminated in this day. We had each, on our own paths, become a part of successful teams. After holding several other positions, by 2005 Roland was once again working with the White Sox as a consultant to the General Manager.

On March 12, 2009, *The Arizona Daily Star* published a story about Roland's career. Roland, now the Special Assistant to the President of the Arizona Diamondbacks, looked back on how "a chance meeting had led to a lucky life." After reading the article, I phoned Roland.

"Arizona Diamondbacks," answered the receptionist.
"I'd like to speak with the Special Assistant to the President,
Roland Hemond," I replied.
"Just a minute, please," said the receptionist.
"Hello," said Mr. Hemond.

Everything had come full circle. Roland recalled our original
meeting and our reconnection following the Sox championship
run. He laughed when I told him that my daughter still has the
autographed photo along with his note framed on her bedroom
wall. "You're giving me goose bumps," said Roland.

He chuckled at the timing of my phone call, informing me
that he was flying to Baltimore, where he and Harold Baines had
enjoyed professional baseball careers following their time with
the White Sox. On this trip, Roland would be inducting Baines
into the Baltimore Orioles Hall of Fame.

I still marvel at my own lucky "chance" meeting with Roland.
For all the changes we experience in life, it is satisfying to find
oneself part of a few long-term teams: the friendships that outlast
the sports season, the co-workers who remain colleagues long
after moving onto other jobs, the friends who turn into family,
and the family who stand by in the best and worst of times.

For the strongest of ties, Team Clock's call to continuously
reinvest is even more profound. We can always choose to venture
forth toward new horizons, with companions we trust and love,
on a journey that is both familiar and exhilarating.

Acknowledgements

This book would not have been possible without the contributions of Mawi Asgedom and Sarah Nun. Our author-publisher-editor team has been a living example of Team Clock at its best. The culmination of this model blossomed from having been challenged and pushed by these partners. The earliest seeds of my work were shaped by my long-time friend and mentor, Randy Lucente. Dr. Lucente introduced me to a developmental understanding of relationships that continues to anchor my thinking.

I would also like to thank the following people for their time and support: Seth Godin, Roland Hemond, Ken Porello, Mike Foster, Bhavna Sharma-Lewis, Dean Simpkins, David Smith, Mike Feinberg, Julie Nagel Hennessy, Andy Plews, Keir Rogers, Bo Menkiti, Joanne Rooney, Jack Eliot, Dan Elliott, Victor Kore, Harold Baines, Cara Cellini, Nicole Francen, Corey McQuade, Jennifer Knuth, Erin McGrath, Elly West, Elizabeth Murphy, Rich Dayment, Jan Clavey, Dennis Nun, Kenneth Wake, Loren Eade, Pete Mockaitis, Andrea Hatch, Mehret Asgedom, Gail Meneley, Stephen Barchick, Shilpa Gokhale, Mike Olander, Flint Dille, and Priscilla Herbison.

Finally, I would like to express appreciation to all of the teams that have welcomed me as a member, embraced our collaboration, and enriched my life.

Train Your Teams

Licensed Team Clock Consultants are available to:
• Host Team Clock workshops for your staff.
• Train your managers and leaders in team development.
• Facilitate team-building discussions at your company retreats.
• Help your organization create a compelling vision.
• Provide phone consultations and coaching.

To learn more, please email us at **info@team-clock.com**
or visit our website at **Team-Clock.com.**

Steve Ritter

Steve Ritter is an internationally recognized expert on team dynamics. His clients include Fortune 500 companies, professional sports teams, and many educational organizations. He is on the faculty of Elmhurst College where he earned the President's Award for Excellence in Teaching. Steve is also the Senior Vice President, Director of Human Resources at Leaders Bank, named the #1 Best Place to Work in Illinois in 2006.

body copy: 11.5/16 pt Bembo Regular
headers: URW Grotesk Medium
subheads: URW Grotesk Regular

printed on 55# natural offset

Designed by Ligature Studio
ligaturestudio.com